498

Fired Up!

Fired Up!

Hot Designs & Cool Techniques for Painting Pottery

KATHERINE DUNCAN

This book is dedicated to the memory of Robert C. Livingston.

Art Direction: Dana Irwin

Illustration: Dana Irwin

Production: Dana Irwin, Hannes Charen

Photography: Evan Bracken

Library of Congress Cataloging-in-Publication Data
Available

10 9 8 7 6 5 4 3 2 1

First Edition

Published by Lark Books
50 College St.
Asheville, NC 28801, US

Distributed by Random House,Inc.,in the United States, Canada, the United Kingdom, Europe,and Asia

Distributed in Australia by Capricorn Link (Australia) Pty Ltd., P.O. Box 6651, Baulkham Hills Business Centre, NSW 2153, Australia

Distributed in New Zealand by Tandem Press Ltd., 2 Rugby Rd., Birkenhead, Auckland, New Zealand

Printed in Hong Kong by Oceanic Graphic Printing Productions Ltd.

ISBN

CONTENTS

Thanks to the owners of "Fired Up Creative Lounge" in Asheville, North Carolina, for inspiring the name for this book.

Thanks to Libba and Tom Tracy, owners of "Goodness Glazes Alive!" in Black Mountain, North Carolina, for opening their studio to us for photos and research.

Over the past several years a new trend has grown out of the ancient art of ceramics which allows anyone to experience the joy of painting and decorating pottery without the complication of setting up a private studio.

"Contemporary ceramic studios," which vary from cozy cafe-sized establishments to multi-roomed storefronts with classrooms, offer patrons everything they need to produce a finished piece of painted pottery under one roof.

The contemporary ceramic studio trend began around 1990 when ceramic artists on both coasts of the United States opened spaces for the public in hopes of making their art accessible to everyone. Today, the number of studios is continuing to grow, and they can be found throughout the United States as well as in Britain, Australia, Canada and Mexico.

The simple techniques taught at ceramic studios allow people of all ages to find a creative outlet. A casual, upbeat atmosphere provides a setting in which even those who claim they "can't draw a straight line" will find an amazing number of simple and inexpensive projects to paint. Studios are often a popular setting for sharing a glass of wine or a cup of cappuccino; birthdays, holidays, anniversaries, and even first dates are celebrated while painting.

This book, inspired by the work being created in contemporary ceramic studios, will make your visit to one of them more enjoyable by teaching you basic ideas about design and color, as well as step-by-step painting techniques. We hope that it will serve as both inspiration and a guide. Take it with you to the studio, relax, paint, and have fun.

Many thanks are due to designers from across the United States who opened their studios and shared enthusiastic encouragement, great ideas, and colorful examples of work for this book. Page after page of finished pieces with descriptions will inspire you with their beautiful, simple designs that range from elegant and traditional to flamboyant and contemporary. After taking up a brush, sponge, stamp, or other tool and trying these sure-fire routes to success, you'll begin to feel like an accomplished artist. Once you try your hand at this art, you'll be hooked!

VISITING A STUDIO AND CREATING A PIECE

Contemporary Ceramic Studios:
WHAT TO EXPECT

If you aren't familiar with a contemporary ceramic studio in your region, look in the yellow pages of your phone book under such headings as arts and crafts, art instruction, ceramics, clay, crafts, glazes, kilns, pottery, and studios. Call your local Chamber of Commerce if you don't have any luck with a listing—most likely, you'll find a studio within driving distance. If there are several choices nearby, consider checking out each one since they vary in prices for materials, studio time, and other offerings. Some studios have a brochure that can be mailed to you listing this information. You should investigate the price range of pottery pieces available, how much is charged for studio time (if there is a charge), and how long it takes to get your piece back after it has been fired in the

kiln. Most owners are more than happy to answer questions over the phone.

Questions you may want to ask when shopping for a studio:

1. What are the costs of visiting your studio? Do you charge by the hour for studio time or a flat studio fee? Does the studio fee only cover a certain number of hours or is it unlimited?

2. How do the prices of your items compare with other studios in the area? (Ask for prices on two or three popular items. For example, you might compare prices on a dinner plate, salad plate, and a mug.)

3. Do you charge for colors? (Most studios don't, but you need to ask since a studio might include three colors and then charge extra per additional color.)

4. How many colors do you offer? Are all of

these available at no extra cost as part of a painting session?

5. Do you charge extra for glazing and firing?

6. Is there a "share charge" for someone who comes along and helps paint a piece during a session? (Some studios charge up to 50% of the project cost for sharing.)

7. Do you allow return visits to complete a project? If so, are there charges for this?

8. How long does it usually take to glaze, fire, and get a project back? (The studio will have to work you into its firing schedule.)

9. Are the underglaze colors and protective glazes that you use lead free and foodsafe? (If you're concerned about safety, check the labels of the underglaze colors and ask to see the label of the glaze. The label should bear a non-toxic seal, have no warnings, contain no lead, and say foodsafe or dinnerware safe.)

10. Do you provide smocks or aprons? (Glazes can stain garments.)

11. Do you have children's rates? Booster seats for them to sit on?

12. Is it all right to bring my own materials, such as brushes or stencils, to your studio and use them?

13. What are your hours?

14. Will you allow me to bring my own unpainted pottery, paint it, and fire it at your studio? (If so, this can reduce your charges considerably if you're painting a lot of pieces.)

15. Can I bring a brown bag with food to the studio, or do you sell food and drinks?

(Some of this information is courtesy of Al Abrams at Ceramicart@aol.com.)

What happens when you visit the studio? First, you'll find an array of unpainted white pottery forms to choose from ranging from standard cups and plates to elegant vases and teapots. Studios offer different selections, so if you aren't happy with what you see at one studio, check out the choices at another.

This type of pottery is called *bisqueware*—the technical name for clay ware that has already been *fired* (baked) once in the potter's oven, or kiln. The heat of this initial firing removes all moisture from the clay, making it hard and therefore easier to handle while painting. (Before it is fired, clay is damp and *green*. Experienced potters work with clay in this state, but most ceramic studios don't carry unfired clay forms or *greenware*.) Because contemporary ceramic studios most often use pre-fired clay forms, you'll be able to paint in a dustfree atmosphere without exposure to the unavoidable clay particles which hover in the air of a potter's studio.

You'll also see an incredible number of colored liquids which look like paints and come in small plastic squeeze-bottles. Clearly displayed and organized by color, these decorative coatings will provide you with a host of shades, allowing you to paint almost anything you can dream up. Known as *underglazes*, these liquid colors are similar to those used by professional potters. All underglazes have clay in them which helps them bond to the surface of the white bisqueware when baked in the kiln. Many underglazes deepen in color or become brighter after firing.

Some studios also have underglaze pencils, markers, or crayons to draw lines, write names, or add shading. But these underglaze products tend to be expensive, so some studios use them only for writing your name on the bottom of the piece. If they aren't part of the offering of the studio you chose, you can buy them at a ceramic supply house in your area where potters buy clay and other materials.

In the studio you'll also find tools such as brushes, stencils, and stamps for applying underglaze colors. The quality and variety of these tools vary from studio to studio. If you gain experience and find that you need brushes or other tools that are different than those provided by your studio, you might be able to find what you want at a craft or artist's supply store.

Pencils and paper will be available for sketching your design and getting the feel for brushing the underglazes or experimenting with a stamp or stencil. Most studios have inexpensive bisqued tiles, which are a great vehicle for trying out different designs and colors before using them on a more expensive piece.

After planning a design and choosing colors and tools, you'll decorate the ceramic piece and leave your items at the studio to be glazed and fired. This means that once you've painted the white bisqueware, the staff will dip your piece in a liquid glaze that contains glassy particles. Your piece will then be baked in the kiln where the heat is precisely regulated, melting and fusing the glaze onto your creation to protect the surface.

The kiln firing will heighten or darken some underglaze colors. Firing times vary from studio to studio, but they usually range from two to four days, depending on how many pieces are waiting to be fired. The studio staff will tell you when to pick up your finished work.

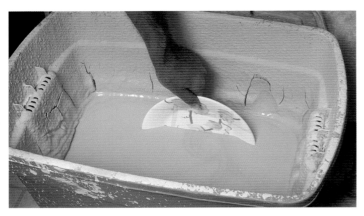

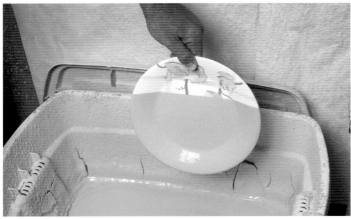

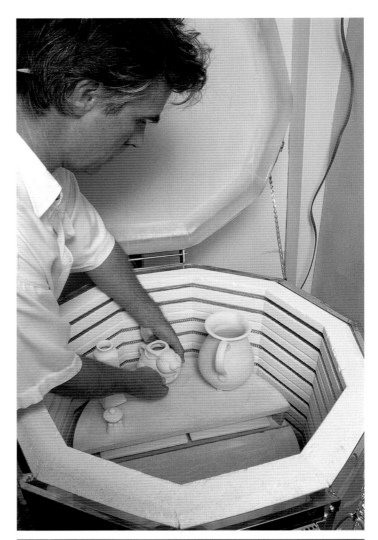

After the studio dips your painted piece in a protective glaze, it is allowed to dry before being placed in a kiln for firing. The glaze changes from a semi-opaque covering to a glassy one after it is fired.

before fire

after fire

WORKING AT HOME

If you want to work at home, many studios are willing to make up a take-out "kit" containing the pottery and colors you've chosen. Compare prices to see if the cost of a kit is considerably more than the studio time that you estimate is needed to complete your project. If you are creating an incredibly detailed, time-consuming piece, you'll probably fare better by buying a kit. Keep in mind that you may have to provide your own brushes and other application tools for painting at home. Some studios sell tools for this purpose.

PARTIES

Most contemporary ceramic studios offer pottery painting parties for both children and adults. These can include birthday parties, weddings, showers, family reunions, office gatherings, and church mixers. Parties usually take place in a special area of the studio removed from other customers. Some studios provide a list of themes, particulary for children's parties.

Others allow you to plan your own party and have it at your home or office by choosing certain bisqueware pieces ahead and adding an appropriate materials fee. Some studios will deliver the materials and pick up the painted pottery after your party to return to the kiln for firing.

When asking about parties, find out exactly what is included, since studios organize and charge for parties differently. Find out if the staff provides services such as set-up and clean-up, demonstrations of techniques, and food. Ice cream and cake, pizza, and even entertainment are sometimes a part of the package.

DISCOUNT TIMES AND SPECIAL RATES

Studios that charge by the hour for painting often offer discount promotional or seasonal times that aren't printed in their brochures. Be sure to ask; you can save on studio fees if you go during these times. Arrive a bit early, and you'll be certain to have plenty of room for a group.

Some studios also offer special rates for children's clubs, schools, and other community groups. Others host fund-raising events as part of their commitment to the community in which they do business. Ask about these options, whether it involves exposing a group of underprivileged children to an afternoon of creative involvement or supporting a local charity through a planned event. Many studios will tailor-make a situation for you.

CLASSES

Check out class offerings at studios. Some studios are more educationally oriented than others and provide a variety of interesting classes for both children and adults on a host of subjects, ranging from basic techniques to painting specific forms. Find out the name and qualifications of the teacher, the price, and how long it lasts. Compare such offerings with ceramics courses offered at nearby community colleges. (You might be able to find a beginning course on surface decoration of ceramics that will teach you more.) Deciding on a class depends on your time constraints, the depth of knowledge that you want to gain, and, of course, your budget!

Sitting Down to Work:
Designs, Materials, and Techniques

DESIGNING

Getting started can be a bit intimidating as you look at a sea of choices of form and color. But as you learn you will find it stimulating to become your own visual composer through using the blank space of the white bisque form.

Own your creation—everyone is naturally artistic if they allow themselves the freedom to follow their imagination without judging how good or bad the work might be in someone else's eyes. Use the ideas of others, but don't be a slave to them. Relax and allow yourself to make mistakes.

Simply choosing a form that you like can lead to design ideas based on its shape. For instance, plates are circular and lend themselves to decorating the rims with borders. This often leads to using geometric patterns, repeated motifs, or designs which radiate from the center. Humans have been using these techniques since ancient times.

Most people prefer to plan their design on paper before committing it to pottery. You can find inspiration for designs from the many projects in this book as well as from magazines, books of paintings, nature, and, of course, your imagination! Look at many designs, let them sink in, and decide what you like and don't like about the examples that you've seen. Do you prefer geometric, straight, and hard-edged forms (such as triangles and circles) or organic, curved, and soft-edged forms (such as renditions of flowers and other natural forms)?

After you've planned your design with pencil and paper, you can draw it directly on the bisqueware with pencil prior to painting it. (Pencil marks will fire off in the kiln and leave no trace.) An easy way to transfer your idea from paper to bisque is by drawing your design on tracing paper (translucent, milky paper), sandwiching a piece of carbon paper between the paper and the bisque, and then re-tracing the lines of your design. You can also sketch a design on tracing paper, rub a pencil over the back of the design to create a solid area of graphite, and create your own carbon of sorts.

If you think you don't know how to draw, begin with the simplest of designs, such as stripes and dots. This gives you the opportunity to experiment with color and learn all the magical things that you

can do with brushes and other tools.

You can also grab a test tile and start experimenting with the paint. You'll be amazed at how a simple idea can lead to others. Some of the best pieces that you'll see on the following pages were invented as the person went along. Stamps, stencils, and other precut forms are great vehicles for this sort of improvisational design—you really can't go wrong.

VASE

INTERIOR - PURPLE

- BACKGROUND OFF WHITE

- CURVED STRIPES

Ukrainian egg designs "Pysanky", with meander lines around edge of plate.

PLANNING A DESIGN ON PAPER WILL SAVE TIME AND ENERGY LATER.

15

COLOR BASICS

"I proceed to a logical development of what I see in nature."

Cezanne

Learning to use color to your advantage is one of the most powerful ways to create dynamic designs on pottery.

Look around at nature and you'll discover everything that you need to know about color. Contrasts of light and dark, and warm and cool colors will begin to become obvious to you. For instance, stare out the window at a group of trees on a sunny day. Look long enough and you'll realize that they aren't simply one color, but many shades of green that vary from sun-spotted leaves that are yellowish-green to dark recesses of shadows that border on blue.

Much of what is called "color theory" is drawn from colors you see in nature. The color wheel categorizes and makes understandable the essentials of natural patterns. Using certain contrasting colors together to give life to your piece will be something that you'll find you do instinctually, but it's helpful to familiarize yourself with the basics of color.

You may have learned some of these principles in grade school. Remember the primary colors—red, yellow, and blue? Many pieces you'll see in the project section of this book use these colors as their emphasis. Together, they create a bold and vibrant look because they haven't been mixed with other colors. They work well for bright, geometric designs with areas of solid color.

An artist may tell you that you can begin with the primaries and mix any color that you want, if you know what you're doing. Mix the primary colors together in various combinations, and you'll arrive at the secondary colors. Mixing red and yellow makes orange; yellow and blue makes green; and red and blue makes purple. Tertiary colors are mixed from the secondaries; for instance, yellow and orange make yellow-orange and blue and green make blue-green.

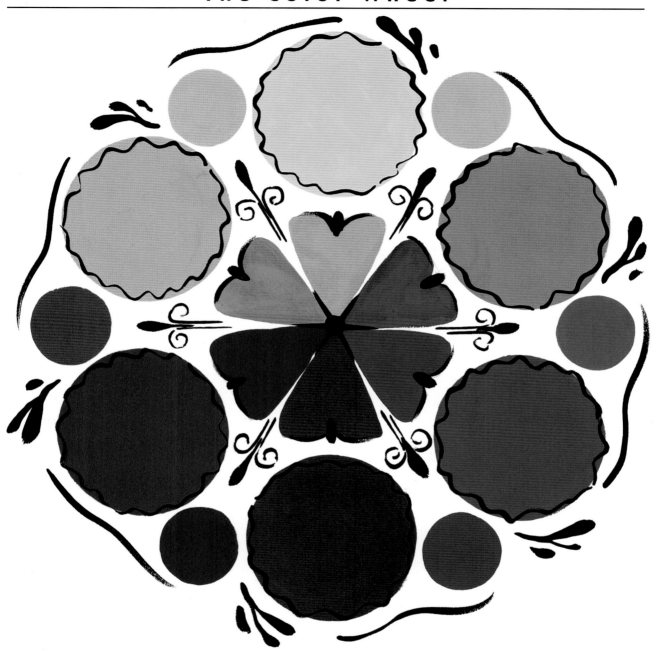

The wheel that is pictured above will show you some basic color combinations that create contrasts. Pick a color and look at the color directly across from it on the other side of the wheel. For example, yellow is across from purple and green is across from red. These combinations are called complementary colors and are used as one of the most effective tools of color design.

Placing these colors side by side will instantly create a sharp contrast that activates an image. Try painting and firing several pairings of them on test tiles, and you'll be amazed at how they affect one another. You don't want to mix them though, because you'll find that they produce a muddy grayish color when combined.

COMPLEMENTARY COLORS CONTRAST SHARPLY WHEN PLACED SIDE BY SIDE.

Complementary colors also represent opposite extremes of light and dark or warm and cool. Red is light and warm, green is dark and cool; yellow is light and warm, purple is dark and cool; and so forth. These contrasts balance one another when placed side by side. Color is usually viewed in context—placing a light color next to a dark one makes it more vivid and dramatic, and pure colors sing when placed next to a dull color (such as bright red next to gray).

You can create movement in your work by using warm and cool colors in contrasting fashions. Warm colors such as red, yellow, and orange tend to advance visually while the cool colors such as blue, green, and purple tend to recede. If you place a bright red flower on a dark green stem, your eyes will seek out the red before they take in the green.

But what about those dreamy, soft pastels that you don't see on the color wheel? Simple—they're made by adding a bit of white to colors. For instance, pink is made by adding white to red, and lavender is made by adding white to purple. Adding different amounts of white to colors, as well as changing the proportions of one color to another, creates unlimited possibilities.

Color is a vast subject, but it can be honed down to some basics which will make your work more effective. As you glance at the many color possibilities available in underglazes, keep the ideas we've discussed in mind. You won't have to do mixing yourself; the studios will offer a host of premixed colors. But some understanding of the basics will help you understand how colors are created and how they affect one another in a composition. As you try out various combinations on paper or pottery, you'll intuitively begin to know which ones work for you. Again, don't be afraid to experiment!

COOL COLORS SUCH AS BLUE, GREEN, AND PURPLE RECEDE VISUALLY.

Applying Color

Painting on bisqueware is much like watercolor or tempera painting—the porous clay surface will suck up the color quickly like paper, creating a somewhat translucent wash. The natural white of the clay will remain anywhere that you don't apply the paint.

To apply underglaze colors, squeeze out a dime-sized portion of each shade that you've chosen onto the palette provided (many studios use tiles for this purpose). Place a container of water nearby for dipping brushes and a sponge. Use a wet sponge to wipe down the bisqueware before applying the color. This step will remove any dust or tiny shards that might interfere with the smoothness of the surface after glazing and firing while giving you a better surface to paint on.

You can create various degrees of translucency and opacity with underglaze color through the number of coats you apply. For thin, almost trans-parent color, one coat will do. Three coats will make your color dark and opaque. Allow colors to dry thoroughly between applications, and apply each successive coat in a direction counter to the last.

A single coat of paint will serve you well if you want to paint contrasting layers of color (such as plaids) onto your piece. You'll have more success if you work from light to dark colors since darker colors will overpower lighter ones. (For example, apply the yellows, pinks, or oranges that you are using first—then add black, blue, or green on top.)

WARM COLORS SUCH AS RED, YELLOW, AND ORANGE ADVANCE VISUALLY.

CHOOSING COLORS

Since colors change after being glazed and fired, most studios provide small colored tiles as samples next to the corresponding bottle of color. These tiles show you what to expect when the piece is finished; use them as your guide when planning a design. In general, remember that colors will get darker and brighter after firing.

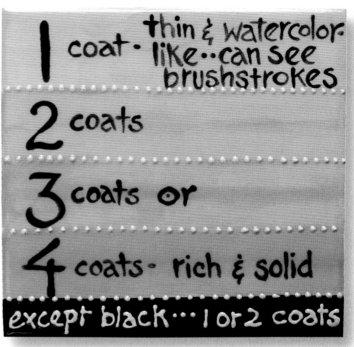

1 coat· thin & watercolor-like··can see brushstrokes

2 coats

3 coats or

4 coats· rich & solid

except black··· 1 or 2 coats

TECHNIQUES AND APPLICATION

Painting Bisqueware with Various Tools

E very studio offers its own collection of tools for application. Many of the techniques you will read about below involve very simple tools. For instance, a leaf can be used to make a print, paper can be cut to serve as a stencil, and almost anything absorbent can be used to

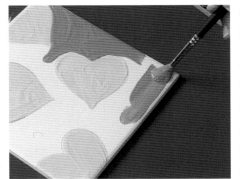

sponge paint onto the surface of a piece. Use the following guidelines, but use your imagination to extend them into new ways of making the surface interesting. Visit craft stores and buy your own stamps, stencils, and brushes. Soon you'll see possibilities in the most common objects, such as using the outlines of your car keys for shapes or a paper towel for pressing paint on the surface. Break the rules, try variations on these techniques, and you'll begin to think like an artist!

BRUSHING

Becoming familiar with artists' brushes and trying them out on the bisque surface is fundamental to your success in painting pottery. Brushes come in all shapes, sizes, and degrees of stiffness. They range widely in cost, depending on whether they are made of natural or synthetic hair.

Some studios believe that brushes are the key to their customers' success, so they provide a variety of high-quality brushes. Other studios supply cheaper, less effective ones. If you find that your studio doesn't provide what you need, remember that you can always take your own brushes (label them with your name so you won't mix them up with the others). Owning a few choice ones will make your experience more rewarding and predictable, sort of like carrying your own bowling ball instead of having to spend time searching the stock for the one that fits your hand perfectly!

Any brush that creates the effect that you want shouldn't be overlooked. Investigate brushes at art and craft supply stores and even hardware stores. Pick them up and pluck them to test how hard or soft the bristles are. Experiment and find the ones that are the most comfortable to use.

The shape, length, and width of the brush determines how quickly the paint runs onto the surface of the piece. Brushwork is used to fill in areas of color, draw details such as outlines, and create numerous other effects that you'll discover as you go along. Learning to use a brush and paint can be both exhilarating and frustrating.

The best way to learn to paint is to test

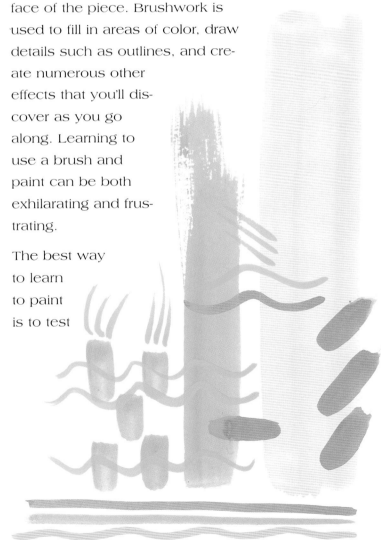

DIFFERING BRUSH WIDTHS MAKE A VARIETY OF STROKES.

brushstrokes on paper. If you want to experiment with underglaze color without risking a piece of pottery, buy some watercolor, blotting, or other highly absorbent paper that acts like a bisqueware surface. Most studios will provide you with paper for designing, but it probably won't be the best for experimenting with underglazes. Take your pad of paper with you each time you go to the studio. This will save you time and money in the long run.

TRY OUT DIFFERENT WAYS OF USING A BRUSH ON PAPER, SUCH AS "STIPPLING" TO CREATE A DOTTED PATTERN OR LAYERING TO CREATE PLAIDS.

Experiment with widths of line, possible shapes, and other ways of covering the surface with brushwork. For example, moving the brush quickly will produce a narrower, lighter line, while moving it slowly will produce a thicker, darker line. Use a wide brush to fill in large areas of color and a small one to create details. Or load the brush with paint and drag it across the surface until dry to create a "dry brush" technique.

You may enjoy a traditional painting technique called stippling. To do this, load up a brush with paint and dot the surface in staccato-like movements while holding the brush at a 90-degree angle. This technique can be used to create the petals of a flower, the leaves of a tree, or patterned areas of design. Juxtaposing and layering areas of stippled dots using contrasting colors (such as yellow and purple or red and green) can make the surface "pop" optically—an idea which is as old as the paintings of Monet and Van Gogh.

SPATTERING / FAKE AIRBRUSHING

To try this fun technique, first cover the surface under your bisque piece with paper. Next, load up an old toothbrush with underglaze color and flick the color onto the surface of the piece using a front to back motion. (You might want to wear a pair of dish-washing gloves to protect your hands from color.) The quickness of your movement, the amount of paint on the brush, and the angle and height from which you splatter the color will create different effects. You can use more than one color and mix them on the surface, or create gradations of color using a progression of shades. If your studio doesn't have toothbrushes, take an old one of your own.

SPONGING

Sponging on underglaze colors with a synthetic or natural sponge creates an easy stippled effect

which can be used to quickly cover the surface of the bisque. Different sponges create varying textures, and can be used to layer contrasting colors. Sponging a very dark color over a bright color on your surface can create a dramatic effect.

Studios may provide sponges which are cut into shapes, such as stars, hearts, and letters. Wet them, squeeze out the excess water, dab them with paint, and press them onto the surface.

STAMPING

Stamping is similar to sponging with cut-out shapes, because you'll use a precut shape with which to apply paint. Many studios have rubber shapes that are precut and mounted on wooden blocks. The surface of the shape is covered with paint and then stamped onto the surface to create a design. These are great for repeating designs, layering, and improvising combinations.

THIS PICASSO—INSPIRED DESIGN COMBINES BRUSHING, DRY BRUSHING, AND SPONGING.

To stamp, brush a coat of paint on your palette

big enough to cover the surface of the block. Press the stamp into the paint and then onto paper. You can also load the stamp with paint with even strokes of a paintbrush.

STENCILLING / CUTOUTS

Stencilling uses cutouts made from materials such as paper, thin cardboard, plastic stickers, and contact paper to mask a design on the surface of pottery. This technique affords you an infinite number

of possibilities for layering different colors and can be used in combination with brushing, sponging, or spattering.

To create a positive form on your piece, simply outline the shape you've chosen in pencil, then carefully cut it out (rough edges will show up on your piece, so use a good pair of scissors). If using regular paper, use a spray bottle filled with water to dampen the cutout. Then press it onto the surface of the bisque with a sponge or brush. Paint over it with color, let it dry for a couple of minutes, then remove the paper carefully with a matt or razor knife. If the edges of

the form are blurry with underglaze paint, you can touch them up with a small brush. This method will leave you with a white shape that you can choose to add color to or leave as is.

Using contact paper can make stencilling even simpler. Just draw the design with a pen or pencil on the plastic side of the paper, cut it out, peel off the backing, and then stick the form against clean, dry

bisque. Paint over the form with color, allow it to dry, and then peel it away. If any of the adhesive remains, simply rub it off with a pencil eraser.

You can also choose to put on a base coat of color prior to applying cutouts. For instance, if

you want to create yellow stars on a dark blue background, simply apply a yellow underglaze coat, allow it to dry, then press the forms onto the surface in the manner described above. Next,

paint on a coat of dark blue, allow to dry a few minutes, and gently pull off the stars. The yellow images will pop right out of your sky like magic. After you've tried the above, using a positive cutout, you can use the paper remains to create another kind of stencil, sometimes called a nega-

tive cut out. The cut-away portion can be taped together to create a complete image of the design with which you were working, so you'll be able to paint inside the paper edges and create any color image you wish. Fill it with color, let it dry briefly,

pull it off, and—viola!—you've got another rendition of the same image.

SGRAFFITO

Sgraffito (pronounced "scra-FEE-toe") is a centuries-old ceramic drawing technique that began with the use of white underglazes over reddish clay which were then scratched to reveal the clay underneath. Greek vases bearing designs created with this technique are familiar examples of sgraffito.

The same technique is used today by professional potters to create intricate, varied lines on their pieces. A simple form of sgraffito on bisqueware will allow you to create lines not possible with a brush.

First, paint the surface. When it's dry, use a tool of some sort (the end of a small paintbrush, a dull pencil, or any tool with a point) to gently scratch off the layer of color and reveal the white bisque beneath. You can use this technique to add dimension to painted letters, texture to forms, and abstract gesture to areas of color. Sgraffito is always the final technique after you've painted the surface, since you are actually carving down through the color to the clay.

To reveal a contrasting color with sgraffito, paint on a base coat of a color with three washes so that it is opaque. Let it dry thoroughly, then apply two to three coats of darker or lighter paint. Remember that you must create a contrast between the two colors for the line to show up on the surface. For instance, paint three

27

coats of bright red on, let them dry, then add coats of black on top. Gently scratch through them to reveal the red beneath.

If the underglaze color curls off the surface as you're scratching into it, wait until everything is dry before removing the excess. After it has dried you will be able to whisk the burrs away with a soft, dry brush.

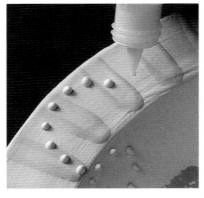

PUFF PAINTS / STAND-UP GLAZES

To add dimensional line to your piece in the final stages, use what are called "puff paints" or "stand-up glazes." These special glaze colors, carried by most studios, are available in nifty little squeeze bottles. They add texture to the clay surface through a beaded line which, when fired, remains in relief on the surface of the piece.

This technique is a contemporary offshoot of a traditional ceramic technique called slip trailing, which was used as far back as the 15th century in Europe. Decorative motifs were squeezed onto the surface with slip (a kind of underglaze) and then feathered at right angles using a comb or feather.

Different widths of line may be achieved by the touch that you bring to the application of the glaze. Moving slowly with the bottle renders a wider line, moving quickly thins it. These paints are often used to make dots on the surface, write names, or create outlines. Like sgraffito, puff paints are usually used as a final technique.

DECALS / TRANSFERS

Some studios have decals or transfers available which can be used on pottery after the surface has been glazed and fired. These can be applied alone on a blank surface or as an addition to the underglaze design that you've created. Decals are composed of photographic images suspended in dried varnish on paper.

To apply decals, soak them until they start to float away from the paper. Gently pull them off, hold them by the edges, and lay them carefully on the surface of your piece. Start in the middle and press outward with your fingertips to release air bubbles. After they're in place, they'll be fired in the kiln again at a low temperature. They can make wonderful decorative additions to a piece, and can be overlapped for interesting collaged effects.

LIQUID WAX RESIST

Special bottled wax can be painted onto areas of a design to shield them from colors painted on top. For instance, you might paint bands of color onto a piece, paint designs on top with the wax, then cover the piece with a black. After firing, the images created with wax are revealed when the wax burns off in the kiln. Not all studios offer liquid wax resist, but it can be purchased at ceramic supply houses and craft supply stores.

Five Easy Pieces

Techniques that we've been describing are demonstrated below through five projects created by Libba Tracy. She teaches them to patrons of all ages who visit her studio (called "Goodness Glazes Alive!") in Black Mountain, North Carolina.

CELTIC TILE

This project illustrates stamping and the use of complementary colors. Notice how yellow and purple sing when placed next to each other.

1

Select a tile and sponge it with water to remove dust. Squeeze a portion of yellow onto a tile palette for use as a base color. Cover the tile with three coats of the color to create an opaque surface and allow to dry for a few minutes.

2

Select a stamp for use on the tile. Squeeze out a portion of purple and paint the spongy surface of the stamp with color. It dries quickly, so apply the color without stopping.

3

Press the stamp onto the surface of the tile with even pressure—firmly enough to release the paint, but gently enough that it doesn't create ridged edges. Adjust the amount of paint and pressure to get the print you want. (It's a good idea to try out any print you're making on a piece of paper or test tile before printing on bisque.) Remove the tile carefully to reveal the printed image.

4

Use a small paintbrush to touch up edges of the image and smooth out any areas where the paint didn't take or is too thick.

5

After the stamped image dries, add purple stripes to the edges with a flat-head brush.

1

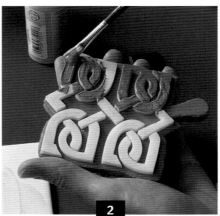

2

3

4

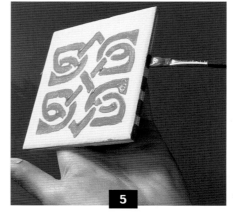

5

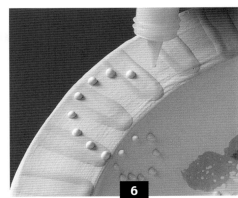

BABY PLATE

This plate uses sponging and puff paints to create a great personalized baby gift.

1

Select several precut sponge shapes. (Original shapes can be created by cutting them out of pressed sponge material which will expand when dunked in water. The star and moon seen here were cut out of this material.)

2

Play with various placements of the sponges on the piece.

3

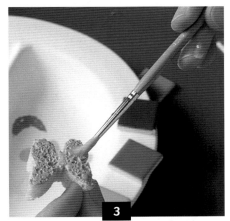

Select colors using glazed and fired tiles and place the tiles on the edge of the plate to get an idea of how they will appear together. Dampen sponges and paint color onto each, then press gently onto the surface of the plate. You can choose to leave a spongy effect after printing or brush more color inside each form. Here, the sponged effect is left.

4

Paint the rim of the piece yellow.

5

Add radiating orange stripes to the rim with a brush.

6

Create a looping line from the butterfly to the rim with dots of white puff paint. Then add buttons, eyes, and a mouth to the gingerbread man. Write the baby's name on the other side of the rim.

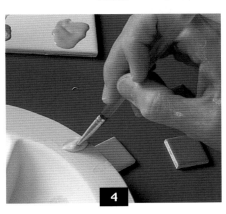

LEAF PRINT TILE

This project uses the simplest of found objects—a variety of leaves found in the backyard. After the leaves are used for printing overlapping forms, a sponge is used to further decorate the surface.

1

After rinsing the leaves to remove some of their repellant oil, experiment with various compositions and decide which one to print. (This doesn't mean that you can't change your mind as you go along, but doing this will give you a general direction.)

2 & 3

After choosing several colors and squeezing out portions onto a tile palette, use another tile palette as a surface to support the leaf. Brush color on the first leaf that will be used for printing. (Use the underside of the leaf for more texture.)

4

Lay the coated side of the leaf on the surface of an unglazed bisque tile. Build the design by adding another leaf coated with red color. Press the leaves gently with the end of a paintbrush to distribute the color onto the suface.

5

Lift the leaves off to reveal the print.

6

Add other prints to the composition with leaves. Notice that a nice effect is achieved by allowing one of the prints to bleed off the edge of the tile. Use a handled round sponge to apply dots of orange by pressing the sponge and giving it a one-quarter turn. This serves to distribute the color evenly. (Notice that the color appears pinkish before glazing and firing. Remember to always reference the fired tiles provided with each color when planning a design.)

7

Use a damp clean sponge to wipe off any orange dot that isn't needed. Areas can be altered with a damp sponge before the color dries.

1

2

3

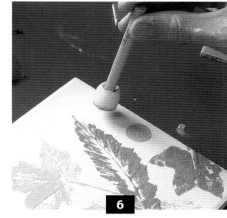

"MAKE A WISH" PLATE

This plate looks complicated, but it isn't once you understand how to use reverse stencils and tracing. The white background created by the bisque creates a beautiful contrast to the colorful rim and letters.

1 & 2

Trim paper cutouts in the the shapes of stars and a moon to be used around the rim of a plate. (Regular paper is used here because it's simple and available, but contact paper with a sticky background is slightly easier to use.)

3

Paint radiating bands of color around the rim. They need not be perfectly aligned.

4

After the base coat on the rim has dried, dampen the paper cutouts with water, blot with paper towels, and press around the rim creating a pattern. If using contact paper, simply pull off the backing and stick the forms to the surface. Using these forms like a mask creates a "reverse stencil." (Compare this with the stencil used for the heart tile on page 35, where the positive area of the stencil is filled with color.)

5

Paint a coat of black on top of the stencils, moving from the center of each cutout outward to prevent lifting the cutouts off the surface with the brush.

6

After the black has dried, remove the stars with a matt knife by carefully probing underneath the paper and then lifting until you can grab the stencil with your fingers. Touch up edges of the stars that are blurred or uneven with a small brush loaded with black.

7

On a sheet of translucent tracing paper, write "make a wish" and draw a falling star with a pencil. Cut this and a sheet of carbon paper to fit the inside of the plate. Place it inside in preparation for tracing the design onto the plate.

8

Trace over the pencil drawing, bearing down so that the tracing paper leaves an impression of the image on the bisque. These marks will burn off in the kiln during firing.

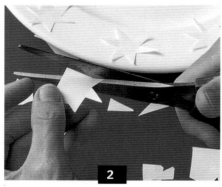

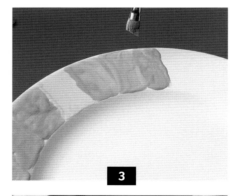

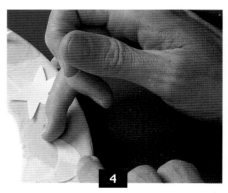

9

Use a fine brush to apply colors to the traced design. Creating letters that are this fine takes some practice with the brush. Try it out on paper or a test tile before doing it on the piece.

H e a r t   T i l e

This tile uses stencilled images accented with sgraffito to make a simple but dramatic image.

1

Use a stencil to trace outlines of hearts with a pencil on the surface of a white tile. (Remember that the pencil marks will disappear when the piece is fired.)

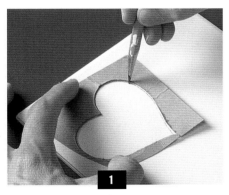

2

Paint the hearts yellow and the background red with two coats of paint. Applying the lighter color first allows you to create crisp edges when applying the darker color.

3

Add black accent lines around the heart shapes with a thin-tipped brush. While the lines are still wet, scratch into the color beneath using the end of a paint brush.

4

After drying, remove any dried splatters of paint (such as the red which was spattered into this yellow heart) with a matt knife. Gently scratch the mistake off the surface, leaving the yellow intact.

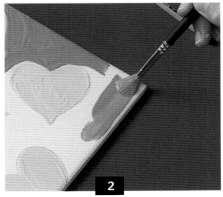

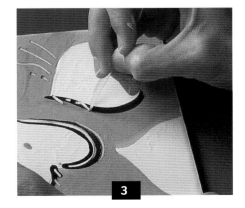

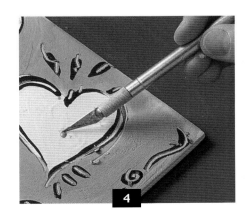

PAINTED POTTERY PROJECTS

On the following pages you will see a variety of designs, forms, styles, and techniques used to decorate the surface of pottery. Designers from across the United States created pieces for this section. Flip through and choose your favorites—look for new ideas to spark your imagination.

All pieces were sponged with water to remove dust before painting. Then they were glazed and fired by the studios after they were painted. Remember, if you are making pieces that you want to use for eating or drinking, make certain that they are glazed with foodsafe materials.

NATURAL INSPIRATION

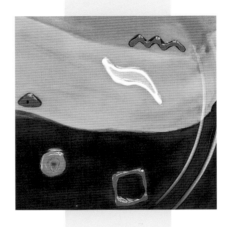

THE PHYSICAL WORLD WHICH SURROUNDS US HAS ALWAYS BEEN A PRIMARY SOURCE OF STIMULATION FOR ARTISTS' IDEAS. THE PIECES THAT YOU'LL SEE IN THIS SECTION REFLECT THE ONGOING RELATIONSHIP BETWEEN NATURE AND DESIGN.

"Leaf Me Some!" Casserole Dish

Design

Robin Swanson

Art and Soul: An Arts & Crafts Cafe! ✦ Atlanta, Georgia

Black, brown, and purple prints of various leaves were layered on the white bisque surface of this rectangular dish to create delicate silhouettes and contrasting areas of light and dark.

Robin applied colors to the leaves with a paintbrush and then gently pressed them on the unglazed surface. A small brush was used to write a humorous message around the rim: "This dish is made with love and leaves and is to be filled with only good things like tuna noodle or lasagna. The only rule is—please leaf me some!!!"

Sun and Moon Coffee Mugs

DESIGN
LAURIE FAYE LONG
MARS HILL, NORTH CAROLINA

Laurie Faye created designs for these two travel mugs using warm and cool colors to represent day and night landscapes. These designs capture the essential shapes and lines of trees and land.

She began by using a flat brush to create vertical background washes of orange and yellow on one cup and blue and lavender on the other. Once the colors dried, she lightly sketched a design in pencil on each mug.

Large areas of color were loosely painted first. The trees were given dimension by painting light green over a deep green. After the areas of color dried, all forms were outlined with lively black brushstrokes.

Patterns of the Earth Plate

DESIGN

ERIN JONES
GREER, SOUTH CAROLINA

Abstract areas of color connoting sea, land, sun, and sky lend the surface of a common plate the look of a painting. Erin began by loosely sketching lines across the plate as divisions for color. Three coats of each color were painted in the divisions to create opaque areas. After the coats were dry, she used stand-up glazes to create various symbols, including an arrow, a star, and a spiral. The remainder of the piece was then punctuated with several dots and streaks of color. The result is a textured surface which has smooth areas of color broken up by small areas of colored relief.

Underwater Fantasy Sink

DESIGN

SHELLEY GODDARD

AS YOU WISH ✦ BOULDER, COLORADO

Finding a turtle and fish swimming in your bathroom sink is an unexpected surprise, but fortunately the ones that you see here won't interfere with brushing your teeth!

This idea is simple to execute. Shelley bought an inexpensive china sink at a home supply store. After planning the design, she cleaned the sink with alcohol to prepare the surface for painting, and then sketched her design in pencil. The sink was then painted with glazes that contain both underglaze and glaze components. Using this sort of glaze, which is glassy after firing, allowed her to fire the colors once without having to add a transparent glaze. (She chose this route because she knew that each time the sink was fired, the risk of its cracking in the kiln would increase.)

The colors were applied by working from light to dark, and the brush was fully loaded between each stroke in an effort to only use one coat of color. The forms were lightly outlined in black with a script liner brush. The rim of the sink was sponged with color in a wavy pattern achieved by dragging the sponge back and forth. White stand-up glaze was used to create white bubbles up the side of the sink.

Seaside Sunrise Bowl

DESIGN

BRENDA STARR
DELAND, FLORIDA

Brenda created this bowl at a studio that stocked greenware—unfired clay forms that are hard, but still damp enough to be carved.

Because she used greenware, she was able to create a scalloped edge by carving away a portion of the rim. The piece was then fired to bisque to

remove all moisture before she painted it. Working from light to dark, she added layers of colors improvisationally, making aesthetic judgments as she went. The swirls

took on their own life, much like the changing hues of the ocean that inspired her. She painted the inside of the bowl in shades of blue and purple to create a sense of visual depth.

Mosaic Tray

DESIGN

MAUREEN B. COLLINS

POT HEAD ✦ CHICAGO, ILLINOIS

Take out your frustrations on a piece of tile with a hammer!

Maureen loves doing mosaic tile pieces because she likes smashing painted tiles and then making a design from the resulting pieces.

To make this project, she purchased a premade tray (available at craft stores), tile adhesive and grout, clear contact paper, and clear varnish.

She began by painting a large round tile to be used for the center along with several extra tiles (for smashing) that repeated the colors of the center. The tiles were then glazed and fired.

The extra tiles were wrapped in a towel (to trap flying bits of ceramic) and smashed. (Test an area with a couple of hammer strokes to see how much force you'll need to break a tile. Begin by breaking one in half, then into quarters, and so forth. Naturally, you won't always be able to control where the pieces break, but experimenting will give you a feel for what to expect.)

After smashing the tiles, she cut a piece of paper the same size as the bottom of the tray. On top of the paper she pieced together her design, leaving spaces between the mosaic pieces. She then removed a sheet of contact paper from its backing and placed it sticky-side-down on the faces of the tiles, allowing her to move the tiles into the bottom of the adhesive-coated tray. Without changing their positions, she pressed them into place, pulled away the contact paper, and allowed them to set for 24 hours in the adhesive. Later, she squeezed grout between the tiles and manipulated it with her fingers to create a level surface. After another 24 hours her piece was dry. (Tiny cracks may appear in the grout after drying, but they can be touched up with more grout.)

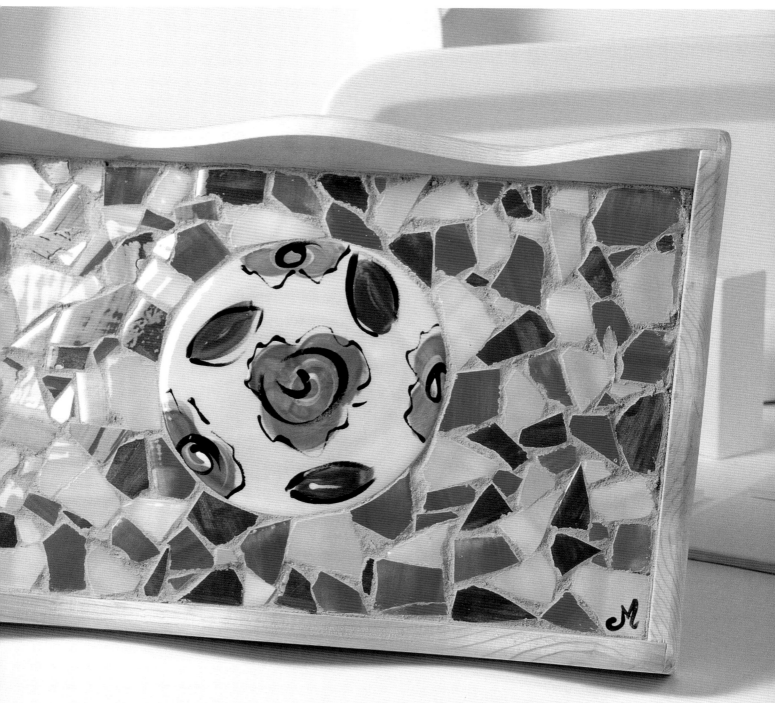

Lemon Bowl

DESIGN

TANA L. H. BOERGER

STUDIO YOU ✦ MADISON, WISCONSIN

Painting bright yellow lemons on a black-and-white checked background with red stripes creates unexpected contrasts in this piece.

Tana began by tracing the lemons in pencil from paper cutouts onto the bowl. She then sketched a dividing line around the bowl as a separation for checks and stripes. Using a flat brush, she painted the checks in three coats around the lemons. Next she painted several coats of bright yellow inside the outlines of the lemon and filled in the leaves with green. She then chose a brush wide enough to create the red stripes and painted them on in several coats. Black painted dots were stippled inside the bowl to complete the design.

Striped Zebra Plates

DESIGN

LEE GRIMES
ART AND SOUL: AN ARTS & CRAFTS CAFE! ✦ ATLANTA, GEORGIA

These simple black-and-white designs are wild and dramatic because of their use of contrast and movement.

To begin, Lee pencilled a design resembling the uneven stripes of a zebra onto the plates. (To make this process easier, cut a piece of tracing paper the size of the plate, draw out the design in pencil, then transfer it to the bisque with sheets of carbon or tracing paper.)

The artist filled in the stripes by using a medium-sized brush to apply three coats of black paint and delineated edges of the design with a smaller brush.

47

Checks and Balances Cookie Jar

DESIGN

TANA L. H. BOERGER

STUDIO YOU ✦ MADISON, WISCONSIN

Getting caught with your hand in this cookie jar will be a pleasure! This eye-popping piece effectively combines light and dark colors, straight-edged and curved lines, and areas of translucent and opaque color.

After Tana outlined a flower and leaf design in pencil, she brushed it with a single coat of paint to create a modulated, painterly effect. She painted three coats of black as a background around the flowers and made checks by using a brush the width of the check desired. (Each check was painted with three coats.) Outlines were firmed up with a small brush.

She painted the lid with three coats of yellow, red, and black and dipped the bottom of a paintbrush in color to make red accent dots as a final decoration.

Tulip Wine Cooler

DESIGN

TANA L. H. BOERGER

STUDIO YOU ✦ MADISON, WISCONSIN

The first warm days of spring bring tulips and picnics. Carry a bottle of chilled wine in this delicately painted cooler.

Tana began painting the cooler by sponging on a background of light yellow. Next, she painted the checks at the base of the cooler with a brush the width each square.

She used a dry brush technique to create the loosely painted flowers. (This technique is done by loading the brush with paint once and dragging it until dry, creating an area with light and dark surface variations.)

She painted the inside of the piece a bright yellow as a visual surprise. (Using the inside of a vessel for color can have a dramatic effect on the appearance of any piece.)

Sushi Plate with Leaf Pattern

DESIGN

MARTI SVOBODA-SIDELNICK
ASHEVILLE, NORTH CAROLINA

This unusual sushi plate is a striking example of how effective symmetrical design and complementary colors can be. This piece is one of the more detailed and difficult in this book, but if you pay attention to the concepts below, you'll be able to do something similar. If your studio charges by the hour, this time-consuming type of project is better done at home after buying a kit.

Marti began with a concept based on the flattening of natural forms into an overall flowing design. She created a shallow, three-dimensional rendition of one of the leaves from unfired clay, then fired it before attaching it to a pre-made bisque sushi plate. This attachment created a little saucer for dipping sushi.

She started by geometrically dividing the square of the plate into quadrants using a flexible paper ruler and pencil. She drew two more criss-crossing lines connecting corners and divided the plate into eighths.

Next, she sketched out a leaf design of a size and shape that could be repeated in each of the four corners. (A stencil was created by folding a piece of paper in half, sketching half of the image outward from the fold, and then trimming the paper to create a symmetrical form.)

She then traced the leaf stencil in the same position at each corner of the plate. The yellow designs which form a cross in the center of the piece

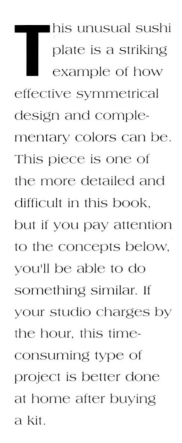

were created in the same fashion by cutting symmetrical paper stencils and then tracing around them.

After establishing the basic outlines of her design with the stencils she applied underglazes with a small bamboo brush to differentiate different areas. (Three coats of each base color were generously applied and allowed to dry between coats.) Next she painted on detailed, raised lines over larger background areas, loading the brush between each stroke. She joined edges smoothly between parts of the design so that no area of white bisque showed through between adjacent colors. She used a bottle of stand-up glaze to draw the final raised white lines.

50

Flowering Plum Tree on a Tea Set for One

DESIGN

SHERILYN TWORK
KINGSPORT, TENNESSEE

This simple but compelling tea set employs one of the oldest painting techniques in the world known as "sumi-e" brush painting or "black-ink painting." Associated with Japanese Zen Buddhism in Japan, sumi-e uses black-and-white line as the essential element of expression. Infinite tonal variations take the place of color. Sherilyn learned this technique while living in Japan.

She painted single brushstrokes to connote essentials of the plum tree branches as an adaptation of traditional sumi-e painting. She explains her method for painting it as follows:

"In sumi-e, the plum tree trunk is traditionally painted with disjointed upright or side strokes depending on the size of the trunk or the branches. The branches are painted with light upright strokes, and the flowers are painted with either an outline or an upright, circular motion in color. I was able to easily achieve all of these strokes with the ceramic glaze. For the flowers, I outlined the shape of the petals and used three different colors of pink. A light pink was used for the buds, and a combination of two darker shades of pink were used for the opened flowers. To emulate the sumi-e technique, I tried to load the brush so that the pink strokes would be visible with only a single brushstroke. In line with a non-self-centered Japanese or Chinese aesthetic, I painted the design on the side which would be facing away from the server if the tea was being poured with the right hand."

VARIATION

Prickly Pear Bowl

DESIGN

PATRICK ALVAREZ
PAINT YOURSELF SILLY ✦ TUCSON, ARIZONA

Even those who feel prickly about painting will have fun with the easy technique used here to create the essential textures of a cactus.

Patrick drew the main lines of the design with a pencil to create guidelines and used a small damp sponge dabbed in light green paint to define the green areas of the pears. After applying another coat of paint, he layered a coat of dark green on top of the light, leaving hints of the light color in order to create dimension. Next, he applied mauve with a sponge to the lower left area of each pear. He further defined the edge of the pear by applying a second coat of mauve, and leaving a gradation of shade in the inner areas. As final touches, he sponged on spots of bright yellow for flowers and added dark green lines to the buds with a paintbrush to give them definition. He dipped the end of a paintbrush in dark green color to apply the dots on the pears.

Simple but Delicious Vase

DESIGN
BILLI R. S. ROTHOVE
GATLINBURG, TENNESSEE

This design was inspired by pieces which Billi admires from early 20th century American potteries.

She began the design by drawing and coloring a thumbnail sketch and then pencilling it lightly onto the bisqued vase. She painted the lighter colors first and alternated with the darker in several stages to create three coats of underglaze. (Small brushes were used for the detailed areas, and a medium brush for the background.) She added accent colors last with a delicate brush.

Notice that the final design matches the shape and proportions of the form on which it was painted—a point to keep in mind when you are planning any design for painting on pottery.

ELEGANT AND TRADITIONAL

  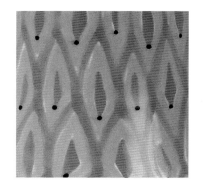

IDEAS ARE PASSED DOWN FROM GENERATION TO GENERATION. IN THIS SECTION, MANY INNOVATIVE PIECES ARE SPURRED BY THE ARTIST'S LOVE OF A TRADITIONAL POTTERY FORM OR DESIGN.

LOOK AROUND! THE WORLD IS FULL OF THOUSANDS OF INSPIRING VISUAL IDEAS—FROM FABRIC TO PAINTINGS.

Garden Plate

LUCY NOTH
FIRED UP CREATIVE LOUNGE ✦ ASHEVILLE, NORTH CAROLINA

Lucy created the beautiful design of this plate by laying out rough circular shapes where she intended to place flowers and fruit. She painted washes of color to create different forms, leaving the background white. Moving from less to more detail, she added the darker colors for stems and leaves as a final touch.

Blue Patterned Plates

DESIGN

ROSE SZABO

WEAVERVILLE, NORTH CAROLINA

By limiting her palette to shades of blue, the artist created unity in the circular designs of these two geometrically patterned plates.

First, Rose drew detailed drawings of the designs she wanted to paint. For the design of the smaller plate, she located the center with a compass and drew concentric circles outward toward the rim to create four bands. (Creating circular bands within which to work provides an automatic frame for repeating variations of a design.) Working from light to dark, she began by painting blue washes of color in the second and fourth bands. She then added light blue radiating spokes alternating with dark blue ones on the first band and painted tipi shapes with dots above them on the second blue band. She continued in this fashion, and finished by painting the dark blue scalloped shape in the center circle.

Rose mapped out the design of the larger plate by dividing it into eight pie-shaped segments using a flexible paper straight-edge and a pencil. (To do this, draw a line straight across the center, add another perpendicular one, forming a cross-shape, and then add two more lines to form and X-shape between the lines already created. Just think of cutting a pie into eight pieces, and you'll have it!)

From the center of this plate she painted each section outward toward the rim and then mirrored it on the other side (creating what is known as a symmetrical composition). She alternated two designs to form the spokes (notice that they are slightly different). Inside the white space that remained after completing the spokes, she repeated a design similar to the ones she had already used.

You can create all sorts of designs by dividing a plate into circular bands or segments and repeating motifs within those boundaries. It isn't always necessary to begin with a plan—just divide up the plate and choose a motif to repeat within the boundaries.

VARIATIONS

Patterned Soup Cup, Saucer, and Bowl

DESIGN

ROSE SZABO
WEAVERVILLE, NORTH CAROLINA

This cup, saucer, and bowl use circular bands and repeating motifs similar to the ones explained for the projects on page 58. For these pieces, Rose used a brighter palette and emphasized an overlapping arc motif and small flowers.

Painterly Fruit Bowl

DESIGN

MARTI SVOBODA-SIDELNICK
ASHEVILLE, NORTH CAROLINA

This striking bowl was inspired by a contemporary painting entitled, "Hunt's Vase," by realist painter Janet Fish. The fruit bowl borrows motifs from Fish's painting, including fruit in a bowl and flowering branches in a vase.

To determine the vertical divisions on the exterior of the bowl, Marti first measured the circumference of both the rim and foot of the bowl by running a string around the edges and then measuring each length with a ruler. She divided each length by the number of vertical divisions in order to determine the spacing between each division.

After establishing two points which corresponded perpendicularly on the rim and the foot, she marked reference points in pencil at spaced intervals around the circumference of the rim and foot based on the spacing she had determined. Next she used a string to connect each set of pencil marks vertically and lightly traced a line along its path to create connecting lines. She

Janet Fish, *Hunt's Vase*, 1984, Oil on canvas, 58 x 36" (145 x 90 cm), Courtesy of DC Moore Gallery, NYC

used masking tape to mask each side of the lines and painted color between the masked areas. This technique created a clean line after the underglaze dried and the tape was removed.

She sketched in the flowers and stems and loosely painted them, following the outlines she had drawn. Using the same painterly style, she sketched the fruit on the interior of the bowl and painted it.

63

Flowering Vine Plates

DESIGN

LAURA ROBERSON
PHILADELPHIA, PENNSYLVANIA

Laura created naturalistic renditions of flowers on these plates by beginning with sketches of real flowers. The wandering vines are effective border motifs, leaving most of the center of each plate white.

She painted the flowers by loading a small brush with color and applying it liberally to form first the petals and then the leaves of the plants. Using a smaller brush, she delicately outlined the flowers in black and dark green. She created the white flowers using only outlines. As a final touch, she painted areas of light and shade on the flowers and leaves.

Madhatter's Tea Party Pot

DESIGN

BILLI R. S. ROTHOVE
GATLINBURG, TENNESSEE

Billi had fun creating the design for this teapot which she says makes her think of the Madhatter's tea party.

She planned her design by making a small, colored, thumbnail sketch before drawing it on the bisqued pot. She then set boundaries for the pattern by filling in part of the design with one coat of the underglaze color. Two more coats of color were applied and allowed to dry thoroughly. With a small brush she added the small black accents.

Paisley Charger and Planter

DESIGN

TANA L. H. BOERGER
STUDIO YOU ✦ MADISON, WISCONSIN

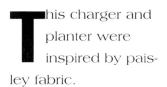

This charger and planter were inspired by paisley fabric.

Tana first sketched these complex designs on paper before she drew them on the bisque. (To reproduce a fabric pattern, outline the pattern on tracing paper and then transfer it directly onto bisque using carbon paper.)

She painted the largest areas of color in three coats to form a background. Then she layered it with tiny dots of paint to create a textured, fabric-like surface. In the tradition of paisley, she outlined each area of color in black, which creates an eye-popping design. This process is time-consuming, but shows how extravagant detail can be achieved with underglazes on bisque.

Cool Water Pitcher

DESIGN

TANA L. H. BOERGER
STUDIO YOU ✦ MADISON, WISCONSIN

The limited palette of this elegant piece is effective because it plays a neutral background against areas of bright color.

Tana created this piece to show her students that they can use almost anything for printing and creating texture. She proved her point by using the most mundane of materials—a mesh carpet pad—which she dampened with color and used for printing on the bisque surface. After creating a criss-cross, beige grid on the body of the piece, she accented it with leaf prints of vibrant red.

Luxurious Soup Tureen

DESIGN

TANA L. H. BOERGER
STUDIO YOU ✦ MADISON, WISCONSIN

The color combinations of this piece create a feast for the eyes—a tureen that's fit for a queen!

Tana designed this richly decorated tureen using the boundaries created by the eight sides of the bowl. She painted each of the divisions inside the tureen with two coats and accented the various colors with dividing lines and dots. Still following the sculptural lines of the tureen, she painted the base and lid.

Stars and Moon Teapot

DESIGN

LAURIE FAYE LONG

MARS HILL, NORTH CAROLINA

The rich colors and fine linear highlights of this teapot were inspired by the artist's love of northern European decorative folk painting.

She planned her design on paper and then cut out paper stencils to trace the stars and moon. Next, with a small round brush, she outlined in black all areas that were designated to have a white background. She painted the body of the pot with four coats of dark blue to achieve extreme opacity. (Outlining the white areas with black helped to keep the coats of blue from bleeding into them.) She added other designs inside the white borders, building from light to dark and creating definition with black lines. After the teapot was glazed and fired, she used a fine-tipped permanent marker to create delicate detail lines.

Checkerboard Fruit Bowl

DESIGN

ELENA DAVIDSON
STUDIO YOU ✦ MADISON, WISCONSIN

The interior of this bowl is emphasized by a painterly design.

The artist created a mosaic effect in the bowl's center by drawing concentric circles with a pencil and a compass and sketching patterns of squares in each of the bands. (Notice the visual interest created by alternating the placement of the squares.)

Moving toward the rim, she applied two coats of red to the middle. She loosely sketched fruit around the rim before filling it with color and outlining it in black. She created a background for the fruit with two coats of bright blue.

She completed the decoration of the bowl with a wash of color on the outside and dots at the top.

Fish Platter

DESIGN

TANA L. H. BOERGER
STUDIO YOU ✦ MADISON, WISCONSIN

The muted reds, blues, and grays of this platter were inspired by the colors of a quaint New England fishing village.

To begin, Tana first sketched the outline of a fish in the center of the platter. (Prepare a cutout and trace around it to make this easier.)

She created the darker outlines of the fish and then added shading with thin washes of color on the body with a dry brush technique. (To do this, load a brush with paint and then drag it until the paint is depleted, creating a fragmented stroke.)

She then used various colors to stipple (dot) everywhere except the rim. By layering perpendicular bands of color in a single coat on the rim, she added a plaid pattern as the final step.

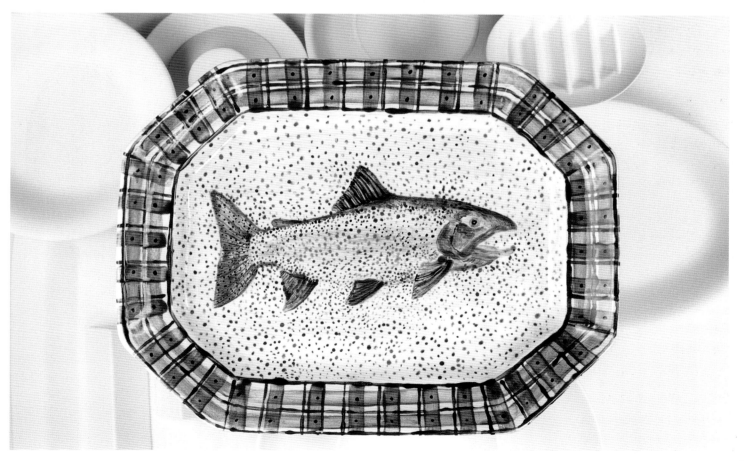

Bud Vases

DESIGN

ELLEN ZAHOREC
CINCINATTI, OHIO

The jewel-like colors of these bud vases were created by overlapping several coats of underglaze.

Rather than following the rule of painting from light to dark colors, Ellen tried painting lighter colors over darker ones. She found that she liked the way a darker color affected the color of a lighter one. The simple dots were made with the end of a pencil eraser dipped in color.

EXPRESSIVE AND CONTEMPORARY

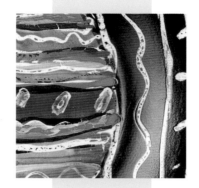
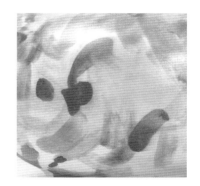

THE FOLLOWING PAGES WILL INTRODUCE YOU TO A SET OF BOLD AND IMAGINATIVE PROJECTS WHICH ARE EXPERIMENTAL AND OPEN-ENDED. MANY OF THEM CUT LOOSE AND BREAK THE RULES— IN KEEPING WITH THE SPIRIT OF MODERN DESIGN.

Cookin' Tiles

DESIGN
LIBBA TRACY

GOODNESS GLAZES ALIVE! ✦ BLACK MOUNTAIN, NORTH CAROLINA

Libba painted these tile samples to show that they can be used alone as decorative pieces or mounted in groups on a bathroom wall or kitchen counter. Tiles allow you to piece together parts to create new designs that cover as large or small an area as you like.

Teapot Cookie Tray

DESIGN

ROBIN CAMPO

ART AND SOUL: AN ARTS & CRAFTS CAFE! ✦ ATLANTA, GEORGIA

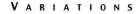

Intentional contrasts between light and dark create the impression of visual shifts on this whimsical tray painted with bright primary colors.

Yellow cups in the background float freely in the atmosphere of dark blue, some of them appearing to leave the tray's surface. By opening the edges of the design in this fashion, the artist created a visual field which seems infinite.

Robin began by sketching and cutting out paper stencils to use for outlining teapots and cups. (Notice the interesting design that he created by reversing the teapot.) To achieve the effects of this piece, he intentionally chose to add coats of color on top of one another while the paint was still wet. As a final touch, he added dimension to the yellow cups with touches of red.

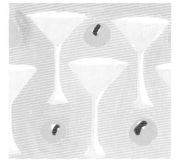

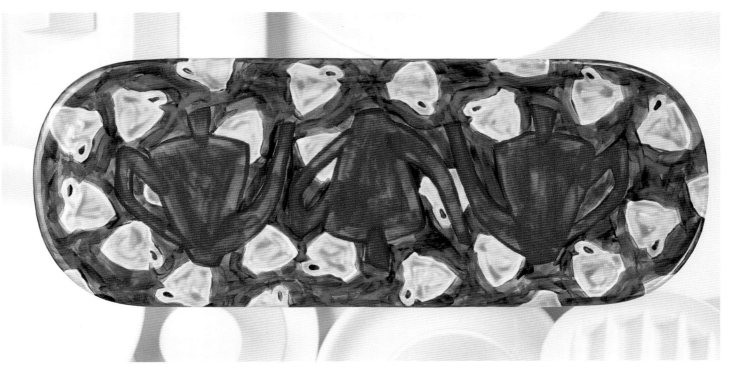

Simple but Stylish Bowls

DESIGN

ROXANNE FRUE / LUCY NOTH

FIRED UP CREATIVE LOUNGE ✦ ASHEVILLE, NORTH CAROLINA

These decorative soup bowls were painted in a jiffy, and they look great!

Roxanne painted the red bowl with green dots by drawing circles on the bisque which bounce between the top and bottom of the edges. She filled the circles with three coats of lime-green paint. After it dried, she painted several coats of bright red onto the rest of the cup, carefully outlining the green dots.

Gold, bright yellow, turquoise, and black make a lively combination on Lucy's bowl. She alternated bands of yellow and gold leaving areas of white between them.

Turquoise stripes were painted down the center of the white areas, which were then decorated with black snaking lines and dots.

Fire and Ice Plate

DESIGN

JORDAN DAVIDSON
STUDIO YOU ✦ MADISON, WISCONSIN

This unusual octagonal plate uses primary colors and black in a simple but dramatic design.

The artist allowed the borders of the plate's edge to determine areas of color. He painted seven sides of the octagon with three coats of red and the eighth with coats of yellow. He filled the center of the plate with a wash of blue, leaving gradations of light and dark. Then he added black lines to define the divisions.

To create the black crackle effect, he loaded a brush with black and trailed the paint toward the center until he achieved the desired line length. He continued this around the contour previously established by the painted black line. To complete the piece, he added dots of color in the center with a small brush.

Mondrian's Soup Bowl

DESIGN

ROBIN SWANSON

ART AND SOUL: AN ARTS & CRAFTS CAFE! ✦ ATLANTA, GEORGIA

A jazzed-up version of minimalism was applied to the round contours of this soup bowl. On the bottom is a humorous comment on the artist's experience: "Robin learns to paint in the lines."

Robin separated geometric areas with masking tape and painted them bright yellow, lime green, red, and dark blue. After the colors dried he added black lines with a fine brush, making them purposefully expressive rather than straight.

Easy Patterned Mug

DESIGN

ALYX HEILIG

STUDIO YOU ✦ MADISON, WISCONSIN

This bright, bold cylindrical mug uses a simple diagonal line to create visual interest.

Alyx sketched the design with a pencil and painted areas of flat color in two coats, leaving blank circles of white in the yellow section. After painting the design, she added black lines with a small brush to divide areas of color.

Stamped Star Plate

DESIGN

TONYA DAVIDSON

PAINT YOURSELF SILLY ✦ TUCSON, ARIZONA

Dark stars against a sunny yellow background represent both night and day in this plate's lively design of yellow, orange, purple, green, and blue. A spiral shape in the center creates a sense of circular movement which is echoed by the orange swirled background.

First Tonya sponged the background with two coats of yellow color applied in a circular fashion. Using a sponge dipped in orange from which excess color had been removed with a paper towel, she created a circular sweep of orange over the yellow background. For the rim, she used two sizes of star-shaped foam stamps to apply one coat of purple, then applied a second coat with a small paintbrush. Using the end of the handle of a

paintbrush dipped in color, she added random dots around the rim. Then she used a spiral stamp dipped in purple to create the center of the plate's design and drew triangles around it with a black pen. She completed the design by filling the triangles with alternating coats of blue and green.

Try technique variations on a plate such as those pictured at the left: use a string dipped in color to print a random pattern, use the end of a pencil eraser to create interesting effects, or sponge a background behind a design that you've painted.

VARIATIONS

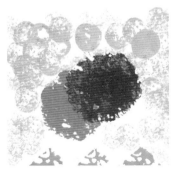

Geometric Patterned Bowls

DESIGN

SUSAN ELLEN JONES
LEICESTER, NORTH CAROLINA

Both of these boldly-colored geometric bowls use primary colors as their basis. The designs fan like wheels from the center, using the circular shape of the bowl as a natural guide. These pieces are good examples of the effectiveness of placing warm and cool colors side by side to create areas that advance and recede visually.

For each bowl, the artist drew and painted a detailed design to determine how colors and shapes would work together. Then she drew the designs in pencil on the pieces.

She carefully painted each area of the designs with three coats of underglaze. She used masking tape to create more exact edges on the areas of the design that had straight edges. If edges blurred when she removed the tape, she corrected them with a small brush.

Mug with Simple Flowers

DESIGN

SUE BUSADA

THE MUD FACTORY ✦ ARLINGTON, VIRGINIA

The simple but effective design of this pretty mug shows how less can often be more.

Sue began by swirling circles of light blue paint onto the white surface, randomly spacing them on the surface of the mug.

After they dried, she outlined the flowers in dark blue with a narrow script liner brush, creating an essential outline to suggest each flower. The handle was painted dark blue, and yellow accent dots were added with the end of a pencil eraser. This design is so easy and effective that it could inspire an entire set of dishware!

VARIATIONS

Rhythmic Vase

DESIGN
MAGGIE D. JONES
GREER, SOUTH CAROLINA

The simple cylindrical shape of this vase is jazzed up with undulating lines of color to create visual movement. A white background with abstract configurations suggests the feeling of modern abstract paintings in which form, line, and color are the subject matter.

Maggie started with a loose concept of a design for this vase, improvising as she went. She established the main lines of the design and then added rhythmic interludes of floating abstract shapes between them.

Modern Teapot and Mugs

DESIGN

JEAN PENLAND
ASHEVILLE, NORTH CAROLINA

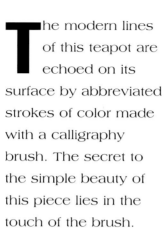

The modern lines of this teapot are echoed on its surface by abbreviated strokes of color made with a calligraphy brush. The secret to the simple beauty of this piece lies in the touch of the brush.

To begin, Jean used a wide brush to paint the floating area of green with one coat of color.

Then she added decorative blue strokes around the rim and body, followed by black marks drawn with an underglaze marker (this can be purchased at a ceramic supply house if not available at your studio).

The artist decorated the mugs below with simple strokes of a calligraphy brush. A black underglaze marker was used to fill in the abstracted human figures.

Black Resist Plate

DESIGN

SHELLEY GODDARD

AS YOU WISH ✦ BOULDER, COLORADO

This piece was inspired by a wallpaper pattern and uses a technique which simulates the process used to make "maiolica" ware.

First, Shelley painted the whole plate in a white underglaze and allowed it to dry thoroughly. Using wax resist, she painted designs on the rim of the plate with a round brush. At right angles to the rim designs, she created squiggles and circles in the plate's center. Over the wax designs in the center, she created various-sized lines with different brushes. Then she lightly outlined several of the lines with a script liner loaded with black glaze.

Next she placed the piece on a banding wheel and began to spin it while applying black glaze to the rim using a mop brush or large square brush. (The color should bead up on the wax. If it doesn't, thin it down slightly with water.) She used a pencil to scratch additional lines through the center lines to the underlying white coat of underglaze. She lightly brushed off the excess color that peeled from the surface when she scratched it. When fired, the wax burned off.

Sixties Retro Bowl

DESIGN

SHELLEY GODDARD
AS YOU WISH ✦ BOULDER, COLORADO

This bright bowl will cheer up anyone's day, whether filled with food or used for decoration.

The artist began by using a banding wheel (a turntable made for painting ceramic pieces) to paint five concentric bands of contrasting color on the bisque bowl. To do this, she turned the bowl slowly and worked from the inside outward using a large brush loaded with paint.

After the bands dried, she painted designs on top of the color 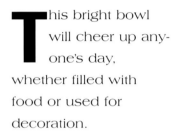 with liquid wax resist and allowed it to dry thoroughly. Next she used a large brush to apply several coats of black that had been watered down to the consistency of ink. (Using thinner color makes it bead up on the wax-resist portions of the design.) The wax created a shield over the areas which later became the bright designs you see on the finished piece. When fired, the wax burned off in the kiln.

Batik Patterned Mug

DESIGN

SHELLEY GODDARD

AS YOU WISH ✦ BOULDER, COLORADO

The intriguing, batik-like, reversal pattern on this mug was created using a wax-resist technique. This is everyone's favorite sort of project—it looks complicated but isn't!

To begin the piece, Shelley painted the handle and rim of the mug bright green. She cut out shaped sponges, dipped them in liquid wax resist, and pressed the sponges onto the white body of the mug between the green bands on the rim. She allowed the wax to dry thoroughly before the next step.

Using a full brush, she applied watered-down black color of inky consistency over the designs in several coats, leaving the green around the rim uncovered. (The thinned color beads up on the waxed portions of the design.) Using a small calligraphic brush, she repeated in black the designs created in wax resist on top of the green borders. In firing, the wax burned off the piece.

Improvisational Bowl

DESIGN

DANA IRWIN
ASHEVILLE, NORTH CAROLINA

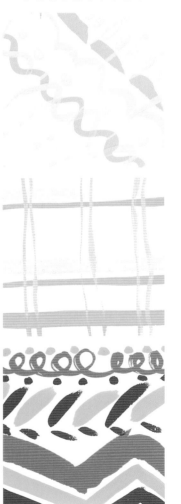

VARIATIONS

Expressive brushstrokes and primary colors were used to make a vibrant design on this bowl.

Dana began by painting strokes of color on one side of the bowl and repeating them around the interior and exterior of the piece. As she built her design in this fashion, more ideas occurred to her, and she added dots or squiggles of color as punctuation. She created a balanced composition by using both vertical and horizontal lines, as well as dark and light colors.

Abstract Expressionist Bowl

DESIGN

SHELLEY GODDARD
AS YOU WISH ✦ BOULDER, COLORADO

The explosive design of this bowl was created by using some surprisingly simple techniques.

Shelley began by placing the bowl on a banding wheel to help her apply paint evenly. After centering the bowl, two coats of black underglaze were applied with a soft, full brush by turning the bowl slowly on the wheel and painting from the center toward the rim. She lightly speckled the center with white by flicking a toothpick dipped in underglaze. Next she used a small, round brush to apply black radiating stripes from the center of the bowl to the rim, leaving a white area of unpainted bisque as a background.

She roughed in the leaves using a round brush loaded with white underglaze. She then dipped a sea sponge in white and turned it at different angles to create a random pattern in the center of the bowl, adding to the white speckled pattern.

She mixed a small batch of gray by combining white and black, and applied it with a sponge in random fashion over the white. When this dried, she used a round brush to paint marble-like veins of white throughout the sponged pattern.

After dipping the brush half in green and half in yellow, she applied color in loose strokes over the white ground created earlier for the leaves. (Painting a white ground first made the application of light colors over dark more effective.)

Dressed-Up Milk Bottle

DESIGN

ELLEN ZAHOREC
CINCINNATI, OHIO

Ellen says that this fun project is almost foolproof. She refers to it as "the kitchen milk bottle of wisdom," because it displays "everything that a domestic goddess needs for a smooth-running kitchen, including recipes, prayers, and lessons that teach children to read and count." And, it can be converted to a vase for a romantic candlelit table!

First, the artist fired a clear glaze onto the bisque bottle, which provided a surface on which to apply decals. After choosing a set of decals, she snipped them into segments, cutting away parts she didn't want. After soaking them to remove the paper, she gently lifted the decals from a bowl of water and applied them to the form in collage fashion. (She took special care while applying the decals, smoothing them carefully to remove air bubbles.) The bottle was fired again at a low temperature by the studio to fasten the decals.

Easy Teapot

DESIGN

BRENDA STARR
DELAND, FLORIDA

This teapot is simple to do and makes a wonderful project to try if you've never painted bisque.

Brenda wanted to create a piece that has the look of her favorite painting medium—watercolor. She chose several compatible colors (greens, purples, yellows, and blues) and put them all onto her palette. Then she chose a brush of the width she wanted and began to add layers of underglaze wash in one coat, overlapping colors as she improvised with short strokes. Because she didn't add more coats of color, the piece retains a translucent surface influenced by the white bisque.

VARIATIONS

Jazzy Soap Dish

DESIGN

SANDY MEKELBURG

ART AND SOUL: AN ARTS & CRAFTS CAFE! ✦ ATLANTA, GEORGIA

Cheer up any sink with a simple, colorful dish.

Sandy repeated strokes of color to decorate the rim and bottom of the dish and then added dots of stand-up glaze on the ridges to provide extra traction for the soap. This piece is a great example of how you can make an effective piece without a complicated design.

FUN PROJECTS FOR KIDS

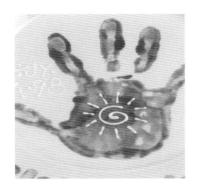  

KIDS ARE USUALLY THE BEST ARTISTS— THEY PLUNGE RIGHT IN AND PAINT WITHOUT WORRYING ABOUT THE FINAL RESULTS! YOU PROBABLY WON'T HAVE ANY TROUBLE CONVINCING A CHILD TO TAKE UP A PAINTBRUSH, STAMP, OR STENCIL FOR THE SAKE OF COVERING A SURFACE WITH BRIGHT COLORS. BUT THE FOLLOWING PROJECTS MAY GIVE YOU AND YOUR BRILLIANT COMPANION SOME NEW THINGS TO TRY THAT ARE FUN AND SIMPLE.

Star Bowl and Bunny Vase

DESIGN

MONICA AND ELIZABETH TWORK

This little vase and bowl were painted with the best tools of all—no specific plan and a child's vast imagination. Squeeze out some colors, grab a brush, and amazing things can happen!

Handprint Plate

DESIGN

LIBBA TRACY

GOODNESS GLAZES ALIVE! ✦ BLACK MOUNTAIN, NORTH CAROLINA

Plates are a much better place for little handprints than walls—this idea can lead to a great project for children of any age.

Libba began by painting a rainbow of color onto her son's hand before he pressed it onto the plate. She added further details around the rim, repeat-

ing the blue found in the center as a final touch. She added stand-up glaze designs in the center of the hand and on top of the rim's blue pattern.

Leaf Outline Flower Pot

DESIGN

CLAUDIA LEE
KINGSPORT, TENNESSEE

Making a piece like this can be great fun.

Begin with an outing in the woods to identify different types of leaves. Gather a collection of your favorites. Instead of ironing them between waxed paper, transfer their outlines to a piece of bisque.

Claudia began this project by outlining leaves with a marker on a sheet of sturdy plastic (a thin plastic place mat or heavy paper will also work). After cutting the shapes from the plastic with a matt knife (scissors are recommended for a child), she traced around the silhouettes with a pencil directly on the pot. She drew leaves on both the outside and inside.

Then she used her outline as a guide and added a couple of coats of color followed by outlines and details. The white surface of the bisque was left as a plain background to dramatize the simple shapes of the leaves.

Santa's Cookie Platter

DESIGN

ELAINE CARPENTER
THE MUD FACTORY ✦ ARLINGTON, VIRGINIA

Leave Santa a treat for all of his hard work on this plate that uses cookie cutters to create a design.

Elaine used her favorite cookie cutters to trace the outlines of a gingerbread man, Christmas tree, candy cane, star, and heart on contact paper before cutting them out with scissors. She then applied them to the dry bisque surface and traced them. (Using contact paper is really helpful for little

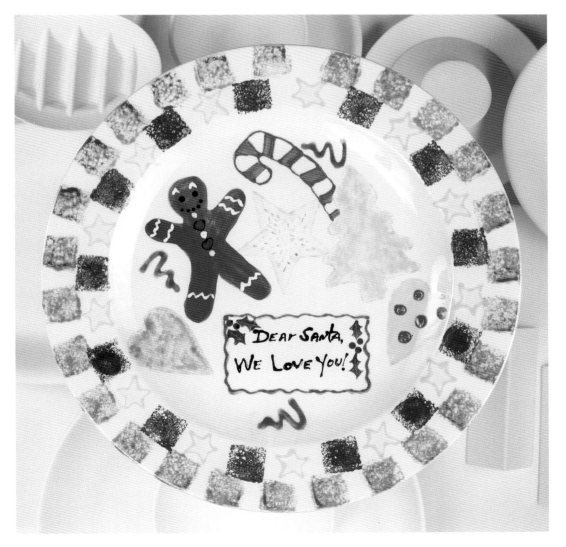

ones because it prevents the paper from slipping).

After removing the contact paper, she painted the gingerbread man and created candy cane stripes with several coats of color. She used square sponges for the pattern on the rim, and then lightly sponged the other outlines inside with color. Using stand-up glazes, she added the lettering and other details, such as the icing on the gingerbread man.

103

"Dog-Gone" Bowl

DESIGN

LAURA HANKIN

ART AND SOUL: AN ARTS & CRAFTS CAFE! ✦ ATLANTA, GEORGIA

Spot will be forever grateful if you bestow on him a personalized bowl lovingly adorned with his favorite treats.

Laura began this easy project by lightly sponging the bisque unevenly with yellow paint. She then outlined the bones with a pencil and filled them in with three coats of color before outlining them in black puff paint.

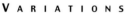

VARIATIONS

Sun, Moon, and Stars Wind Chimes

DESIGN

AMI MATHEWS
THE MUD FACTORY ✦ ARLINGTON, VIRGINIA

This charming set of wind chimes was produced from a surplus of round bisque forms purchased for use as Christmas ornaments. This idea has many possibilities—you can vary the designs, the number of discs that you use, and their configuration. As the owner of this studio tells her patrons, "learn to think out of the box!"

After Ami determined her design by lightly sketching the outlines of the stars and moon on two discs, she painted them with three coats of yellow followed by blue for the background. (She left small sections of background white for the eyes and mouth.) She added outlines with a small brush.

After drying, she lightly sponged the reverse sides of the discs (two of which are pictured) with paint and decorated them with small painted stars. Using gold wrapping cord (any kind of string,

cord, ribbon, or monofilament will work), she strung the finished discs onto a sturdy twig.

Crocodile Plate

DESIGN

AMBER MOODY
AS YOU WISH ✦ BOULDER, COLORADO

Peas seem to be universally unpopular with kids, and this plate makes light of the notion that they'll never disappear.

Amber created these cavorting crocodiles by sketching the designs onto a plate with a pencil and then filling in the bodies with green underglaze. She used a small brush to add outlines, details, and words. (The details could also be done using black stand-up glaze squeezed from a bottle.)

Best Friends Plate

DESIGN

SHARON DICKERSON
PAINT YOURSELF SILLY ✦ TUSCON, ARIZONA

This project uses the outlines of a t-shirt transfer (this one created by Glick Publishing) to decorate a plate. Any image can be traced with the technique used here.

Sharon selected her design and then fixed it to the plate with masking tape at the top. She then slipped transfer paper (carbon paper works, too) between the design and bisque, and traced the design onto the bisque with a pencil (the traced lines will burn off in the kiln later). She filled in the larger areas with two to three coats of color, and then outlined the design and letters with stand-up black glaze.

"Brandtasaurus Rex" Plate

DESIGN

DREW DAVIDSON

PAINT YOURSELF SILLY ✦ TUSCON, ARIZONA

Dinosaurs continue to fascinate kids, and this plate plays on the name of a dinosaur—"brontosaurus rex"—by using Brandt's name. (Any child's name can be substituted.)

Drew created this plate by choosing a set of pre-made stickers of dinosaurs (these are made by "Stickopotamus," but you can use any type) which he then applied around the rim. He painted three coats of yellow background color over them and allowed them to dry.

After removing the stickers, he rubbed off bits of adhesive which were left on the bisque by using a pencil eraser. He then painted three coats of paint with a small paintbrush inside the outlines left by the stickers. He added lettering with a black ballpoint pen and black stand-up glaze.

Hearts, Flowers, and Special Occasions

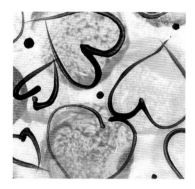 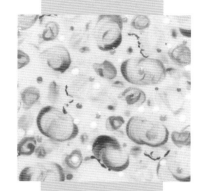 

BE SENTIMENTAL, FUNNY, OR BOLD BY EXPRESSING YOUR FEELINGS FOR SOMEONE YOU CARE ABOUT THROUGH A PIECE OF PAINTED POTTERY MADE ESPECIALLY FOR THEM. CELEBRATE HOLIDAYS AND SPECIAL DAYS WITH PERSONALIZED GIFTS AND SEASONAL DECORATIONS. HAVE A THEME PARTY TO SHOW OFF YOUR CREATIONS— YOUR FRIENDS WILL BE AMAZED AT YOUR FLAIR!

Heart Plate

DESIGN

SHELLEY GODDARD
AS YOU WISH ✦ BOULDER, COLORADO

Shelley created this simple design by dipping round sponges-on-a-stick in several shades of red and pressing them randomly on the plate. (You can use several sponges or one can be rinsed with water and reused between each application.) She made a random pattern by using a small brush to loosely outline the shapes she had sponged. It's that easy!

VARIATIONS

Heart Nesting Bowls

DESIGN
ELLEN ZAHOREC
CINCINNATI, OHIO

This colorful set of bowls was created by painting and then sponging. Ellen chose to use contemporary "southwestern" colors because she liked the idea of updating a traditional design and form.

First she painted contrasting bands of color (blue, red, orange, and turquoise) in three smooth coats around the rim and body of each bowl. Using heart and star-shaped sponges, she followed the form of the bowl and added shapes on top of the dry color by sponging. She worked from both light to dark and dark to light, enjoying the way the background color altered the applied color (notice the differences on the smallest bowl between the red hearts on the rim and those sponged inside the bowl). After firing, the colors deepened, creating a rich, opaque look.

Small Pitcher with Flowers

DESIGN

LIBBA TRACY

GOODNESS GLAZES ALIVE! ✦ BLACK MOUNTAIN, NORTH CAROLINA

Libba created the design of this graceful pitcher by first using a dry brush technique to layer areas of pink and yellow in a single coat onto the body of the piece. After this coat dried, she painted pink flowers in circular shapes that were then defined by scratching out the contours with the end of a paint-brush. She used turquoise to outline leaves, allowing the background colors to show through.

Cupid Pitcher

DESIGN

SHELLEY GODDARD

AS YOU WISH ✦ BOULDER, COLORADO

This unusual take on a traditional theme is enhanced by cupids which disappear behind bright stripes of color. How is this magic trick accomplished? Read on!

Shelley began by painting the body of the pitcher with bright stripes of yellow using a brush the width of the stripe. Then she painted the handle yellow. After the yellow dried, she painted the spout, inside, and bottom rim dark blue and added stripes of dark blue on the handle, covering the yellow. For contrast, she later dotted yellow paint on top of the dark blue spout. The piece was then glazed and fired.

She added cupid decals to the glazed surface. (The ones that peep out are created by simply cutting the decals in half to create the illusion of a disappearing cupid.) The piece was then fired again at a low temperature to fasten the decals to the surface. (Decals are considered to be an "over-the-glaze" technique in ceramics.)

Hearts and Flowers Plate

DESIGN

SHELLEY GODDARD
As You Wish ✦ Boulder, Colorado

The confectionary look of this plate makes it a sweet gift for a wedding, Mother's Day, or any sentimental occasion.

The artist began by sketching a simple heart in the center of the plate. (Cut out a stencil and trace the heart if you aren't this brave!)

Ruby, turquoise, bright yellow, orange, and green were selected for the palette, and she began by swirling the larger flowers onto the plate in a random pattern with a small to medium round brush. (To do this, place the loaded brush on the surface and turn it clockwise to create a circle.) Next she used the tip of her smallest finger to dip the yellow and orange paint and dot on smaller yellow flowers. Using a pencil eraser dipped in turquoise, she randomly dotted on more flowers to complete the design.

Dotting the paint in this fashion created a beautiful textured surface.

Bee and Flower Plate

DESIGN

ELAINE CARPENTER
THE MUD FACTORY ✦ ARLINGTON, VIRGINIA

This delicate design is achieved by using masking, sponging, and stamping. The simple trail of the bee created with stand-up glaze adds visual movement to the piece.

Elaine began by cutting the outlines of two flowers from contact paper that were then pressed against a clean, dry bisque surface. She sponged a light purple over the entire plate to create a background and then removed the contact paper to reveal white flowers. Next, she used a sponge in the shape of a leaf to add light and dark green petals to the flowers and around the rim where dots of blue paint form the center of the leaf clusters. She further defined the white flowers by lightly adding color with a sponge cut in the same shape. She added final details with a brush and stand-up glaze.

Updated Flower Basket

DESIGN

ELLEN ZAHOREC
CINCINNATI, OHIO

This ornamental flower basket updates a traditional form through the use of bright, contemporary colors. Ellen used complementary colors, such as orange and blue and yellow and purple, to create contrast and drama.

The artist used the preformed shape of the basket to determine the borders of her design. She used three coats of paint applied with fine brushes—a time-consuming process. From this experience, she noted that it was important to be conscious of how many coats of paint were applied to a certain area, because it was easy to lose track.

She suggested making a quick sketch on paper of the areas to be painted before beginning, and then making note of the number of coats.

This is a project for a person with time, a steady hand, and patience—but the outcome is well worth the effort!

Flowered Wine Cooler or Vase

DESIGN

ELLEN ZAHOREC

CINCINNATI, OHIO

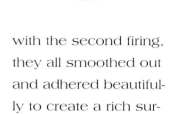

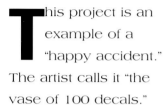

This project is an example of a "happy accident." The artist calls it "the vase of 100 decals."

Ellen began with the idea of applying a few decals of flowers to an already-glazed surface, but after applying the decals and firing them, she found that they bubbled and created a rough surface. (This probably happened either because she didn't smooth out all of the decals when she applied them or they were fired at too high a temperature.) She thought that the piece was ruined, but decided to try something.

Instead of throwing it away, she layered more decals on top, creating an interesting and complex overlapping pattern of flowers. The second time, she was very careful to press out all bubbles from the decals, and, with the second firing, they all smoothed out and adhered beautifully to create a rich surface. Eureka!

"Will You Marry Me?" Plate

DESIGN

MELANIE MAREN
AS YOU WISH ✦ BOULDER, COLORADO

As your beau approaches the end of a delicious meal you've prepared, he'll be in for an even bigger surprise than your culinary skills! Ask for anything you dare to—using the simple techniques that Melanie used.

First, she painted her message in the center of the plate with a script liner brush. Then she used a medium-sized flat brush to paint the center rim with a checkerboard design (the brush was the width of each square). After these areas dried, she painted wax resist over the lettering and the checkerboard rim. She painted hearts directly onto the bisque surface of the outer rim with wax resist. She added the vines between the hearts with wax painted with a liner brush and applied the small dots with the end of a paintbrush handle dipped in wax resist.

Next, with a large soft brush she painted on two coats of red in the center and on the rim of the piece. (The color doesn't cover the waxed areas, but beads up on them.) After the piece was fired, the wax melted and left Melanie's message.

"Light Up My Life" Switchplates

DESIGN

ELLEN ZAHOREC
CINCINNATI, OHIO

These cute switch-plates use the simple outline of a heart as their motif.

Ellen sketched a heart on each switchplate (use a cut stencil if you want a perfect heart)

and then painted them with three coats of red underglaze. Following the outline of the plate with a brush close to the width desired, she created borders around the plates.

After several coats of underglaze were applied and dry, she used stand-up glazes (puff paints) to make raised dots on the border.

"Ole, Mole!" Chip and Dip Platter

DESIGN

BROOKE KELLY

ATLANTA, GEORGIA

This festive chip-and-dip bowl uses ribbons of color on a background of bright yellow, suggesting hot climates and spicy food.

Brooke began this piece with four colors that worked well to express her idea of a flamboyant summer party. She painted the whole platter bright yellow by loading a mop brush with paint and then turning the platter slowly on a turntable. Three coats of paint gave her an opaque surface on which to paint other bands of color. She then layered on her other colors, taking advantage of the life that the yellow base coat gave to green, brown, and maroon.

She painted the center spiral by loading a small brush with paint and turning the platter while slowly expanding the circumference of a circle. For final festive touches, she used a narrow brush and all the colors of her palette to paint lively "streamers" that seem to pop against the yellow background.

Watermelon Pitcher

DESIGN

KRIS HOLMES
PAINT YOURSELF SILLY ✦ TUCSON, ARIZONA

Wet your whistle from this juicy pitcher during Fourth of July celebrations, barbeques, and lazy summer afternoons on the porch.

An easy project for the inexperienced, it involves applying darker colors over lighter ones to create a surface that resembles the spongy fruit of the watermelon and its rind. Kris used sea sponges to apply the paint on this piece, but you can achieve similar effects with synthetic sponges.

On the top portion of the pitcher the artist sponged two coats of pink on white bisque followed by two coats of red. She left a band of white between the red and the green, then sponged light green on the bottom half in two coats, followed by one coat of dark green. She randomly drew and placed seeds with a pen, then filled in the outlines with two coats of black.

Pysanka Plate

DESIGN

MARK SIDELNICK

ASHEVILLE, NORTH CAROLINA

The art of "pysan-ka"—painting intricate symbolic designs on eggs—is thousands of years old and practiced in the Ukraine today. This plate design, inspired by the artist's heritage, contains many traditional symbols, including the circle, which represents the cyclical nature of the universe, and the horse, which represents wealth, prosperity, endurance, and speed.

The design has four quadrants, each of which contains an egg. To divide the plate into sections, Mark found the center of the plate using a compass and created concentric circles to define the bands. Next, he divided the plate into four quadrants by drawing a line through the center with a flexible ruler and another through the center at a right angle to form a cross. He created an egg-shaped paper stencil and traced it four times using the crossing lines as a guide.

Next, he outlined the shapes inside the egg in pencil using small paper stencils to create even edges. He painted three coats of color into each detailed section for an opaque effect. (Masking tape comes in handy for masking different areas and keeping straight lines on a design such as this.) The background was left white, creating a crisp contrast for the bright colors he chose. He added the final raised lines, including the distinct outlines of the eggs, with stand-up glazes.

Violin Plate

DESIGN

JENNIFER BISTRAK

ART AND SOUL: AN ARTS AND CRAFTS CAFE ✦ ATLANTA, GEORGIA

Strings are by far the most romantic of instruments—bringing to mind beautiful moonlit evenings and strolling musicians.

This lyrical design was painted by the artist with a limited palette of brown, blue, and black. He began by sketching a loose outline of the design on bisque, leaving white space around the violin to form a shape that echoes its curves. After layering several coats of color to form the blue border and the violin, he outlined curves and a bow with expressive black lines painted with a small brush.

124

Woman Rising Vase

DESIGN
BRENDA STARR
DeLand, Florida

This vibrant piece was created as a tribute to women. The elliptical shape of the vase gave Brenda a surface on which to pursue a two-dimensional design.

The artist found this unusual vase in a studio that stocked unfired clay forms, or greenware. Because a greenware form is dry to the touch but still contains enough moisture to carve, she was able to cut away parts of the rim to create a curving pattern and then carve her design into the surface with the tip of a large, sharp nail. The piece was then fired to bisque by the studio, removing all moisture from the clay and hardening it.

On the white bisque surface she applied washes of color to correspond to the design which she had outlined by carving. She used single coats to create a translucent, watercolor effect.

Notice the way she used graduated areas of color, moving from darker areas of paint to light or even white, in order to create fans of light and shade. Areas of white were left to convey many parts of her design.

Christmas Tree Treat Dish

DESIGN

LIBBA TRACY

GOODNESS GLAZES ALIVE! ✦ BLACK MOUNTAIN, NORTH CAROLINA

A pre-formed Christmas tree shape makes a wonderful surface to decorate with any ornaments that you can dream up.

Libba painted a traditional tree by using several coats of dark green to form a background for swags and ornaments created by using stand-up glazes. Beads of color formed by the glaze squeezed from small bottles make perfect jewel-like ornaments that catch the light after glazed and fired. Libba painted a tiny present at the base of the tree as a final, imaginative addition to this festive holiday dish.

Father's Day Platter

DESIGN

MELANIE MAREN
AS YOU WISH ✦ BOULDER, COLORADO

Tease your dad with this plate that sports two tempting fish.

To begin this project, Melanie sketched the design in pencil. She used brushed translucent washes to fill in and overlap areas of color suggesting the shapes of the fish. She added more color and definition on top of the base coat with brushstrokes suggesting fins, a tail, and a body. Using the end of a paintbrush, she scratched sgraffito lines onto the surface of the fish to further define details. She used stand-up black glaze to create the lettering and the hook and line. (Differing widths can be made by increasing or decreasing the pressure on the glaze bottle.)

She then placed the piece on a banding wheel for "fake airbrushing," or splattering. After loading a toothbrush with black paint, she spun the plate on the wheel and plucked the brush to release speckles of paint from four to six inches away. She finished the plate by sponging the edge with black while turning it on the wheel.

Index